Watch It Grow

A Bean's Life

Nancy Dickmann

Heinemann Library
Chicago, Illinois

www.heinemannraintree.com

Visit our website to find out more information about Heinemann-Raintree books.

To order:

☎ Phone 888-454-2279

🖥 Visit www.heinemannraintree.com to browse our catalog and order online.

Edited by Rebecca Rissman, Nancy Dickmann, and Catherine Veitch
Designed by Joanna Hinton-Malivoire
Picture research by Mica Brancic
Production by Victoria Fitzgerald
Originated by Capstone Global Library Ltd
Printed and bound in China by South China Printing Company Ltd

14 13 12 11 10
10 9 8 7 6 5 4 3

Library of Congress Cataloging-in-Publication Data
Dickmann, Nancy.
  A bean's life / Nancy Dickmann. -- 1st ed.
    p. cm. -- (Watch it grow)
  Includes bibliographical references and index.
  ISBN 978-1-4329-4142-0 (hc) -- ISBN 978-1-4329-4151-2 (pb) 1. Beans--Life cycles--Juvenile literature. I. Title. II. Series: Dickmann, Nancy. Watch it grow.
  QK495.L52D54 2010
  583'.74--dc22
                                2009049158

Acknowledgments
We would would like to thank the following for permission to reproduce photographs: Corbis pp. **4** (Flame/© Tim Pannell), **7** (© Gary K Smith), **12** (Photoconcepts/© Bill Holden); FLPA pp. **13** (© Gary K Smith); Getty Images p. **19** (FoodPix/Sandra Ivany); iStockphoto pp. **6** (© quidnunc), **10** (redmal), **18** (floortje), **20** (RawFile), **22 top** (© quidnunc), **22 left** (floortje), **22 right** (redmal), **23 top** (floortje), **23 middle top** (Arlindo 71), **23 bottom** (redmal); Nature Picture Library p. **17** (© Adam White); Photolibrary pp. **5** (Flirt Collection/Corbis), **8** (Imagestate RM/© Gary Smith), **9** (© Oxford Scientific (OSF)), **14** (Garden Picture Library/© Maxine Adcock), **15** (Garden Picture Library/© Howard Rice), **21** (© Oxford Scientific (OSF)), **22 bottom** (Garden Picture Library/© Howard Rice), **23 middle bottom** (© Oxford Scientific (OSF)); Shutterstock p. **11** (Marek Pawluczuk); **16** (Jo Stafford).

Front cover photograph (main) of harvested broad beans reproduced with permission of iStockphoto (© Frederique Catherine Jones). Front cover photograph (inset) of bean shoots reproduced with permission of Shutterstock (© Filipe B. Varela). Back cover photograph of a bean shoot reproduced with permission of iStockphoto (redmal).

The publisher would like to thank Nancy Harris for her assistance in the preparation of this book.

Every effort has been made to contact copyright holders of material reproduced in this book. Any omissions will be rectified in subsequent printings if notice is given to the publisher.

Contents

Life Cycles

All living things have a life cycle.

A bean has a life cycle.

A bean is a seed. It grows into a new bean plant.

The bean plant grows beans.
The life cycle starts again.

Seeds and Shoots

A bean grows in the ground.

root

Roots grow down from the seed into the ground.

shoot

A shoot grows from the bean.

leaves

Leaves grow from the shoot.

Becoming a Bean Plant

The bean plant makes its own food from water, sunlight, and air.

The bean plant grows bigger.

The bean plant grows flowers in the spring.

flower

The flowers are white with dark spots.

Making Seeds

A bee comes to feed on a flower.
The bee has pollen on it.

new bean

The pollen helps make new beans grow on the plant.

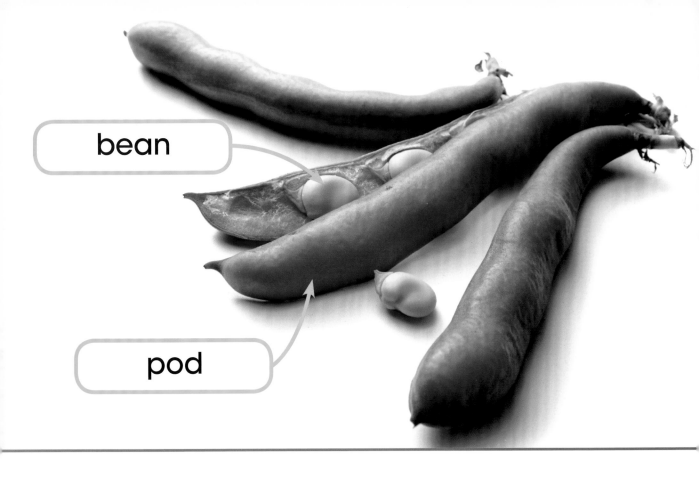

bean

pod

The beans grow inside a pod.

The pods look lumpy when the beans are grown.

Some beans fall to the ground.

The life cycle starts again.

Life Cycle of a Bean Plant

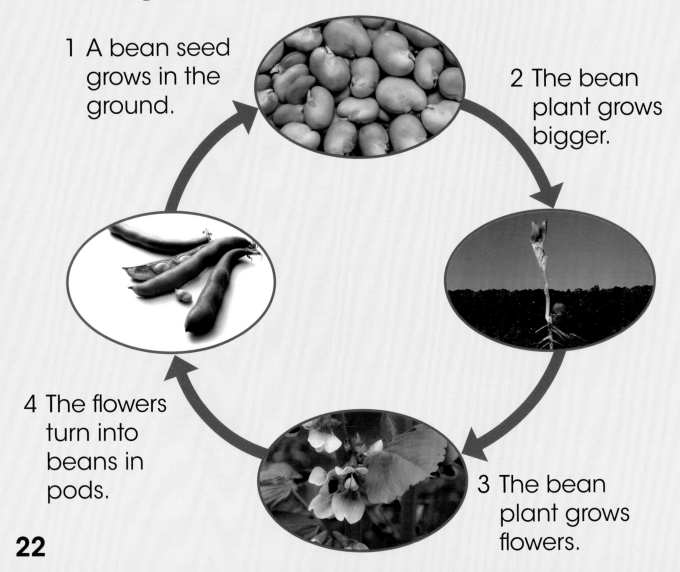

1 A bean seed grows in the ground.

2 The bean plant grows bigger.

3 The bean plant grows flowers.

4 The flowers turn into beans in pods.

22

Picture Glossary

pod tough outer case that protects seeds such as beans

pollen yellow powder inside a flower

root part of a plant that grows underground. Roots take up water for the plant to use.

shoot small green stem that grows from a seed

23

Index

Notes to Parents and Teachers

Before reading

Show the children a broad bean pod and ask if they know what's inside. Hand out some pods and get them to open them up and look at the beans. Ask the children if they have ever grown beans. Do they like to eat them?

After reading

- Give each child an empty yogurt pot, some soil, and a broad bean to plant. Make sure they keep their pots in sunlight and water the growing plants regularly. If your school has a garden, move the plants outside when they are big enough.
- Do some broad bean math problems together. Collect some broad bean pods and measure them. How long is the biggest pod? How long is the smallest? Can the children guess how many beans are in each pod? Open up the pods and count the number of beans. Are there more beans in the longest pod?
- Read Jim and the Beanstalk by Raymond Briggs.

24